Appalachian Trail

Jeanne Wallace-Weaver

Contents

Let's Go on a Hike

Sometimes people take vacations in the **wilderness**, far from cities and towns. They might **hike**, or walk, through forests and over mountains. People who hike in the wilderness for days or months must carry the things they need on their backs. Imagine dragging a kitchen and a bed through the woods. It doesn't seem possible! Yet each year this is what thousands of people do when they hike the Appalachian Trail.

Hikers walk in Acadia National Park in Maine.

The Appalachian Trail, or A.T., is a 2,172-mile **footpath**. The trail follows the Appalachian Mountains, a long **mountain range** in the eastern United States. The mountain range runs from Alabama to Canada. The A.T. passes through a number of states from Georgia all the way to Maine!

Hikers along the A.T. cross rivers, climb mountains, hike down into valleys, and pass over roads. They look at trees, flowers, and animals. They rest by waterfalls, and sleep under the stars.

How many miles would an A.T. hiker walk from this sign to Mount Katahdin?

NEWFOUND GAP

ELEVATION 5,045
APPALACHIAN TRAIL

BOULEVARD TRAIL	2
ICE WATER SPRINGS	3
THE JUMP–OFF	3
CHARLIE'S BUNION	4
MT. LECONTE	8
DAVENPORT GAP	30
VA./TENN. (DAMASCUS)	194
MT. KATAHDIN (MAINE)	1,823

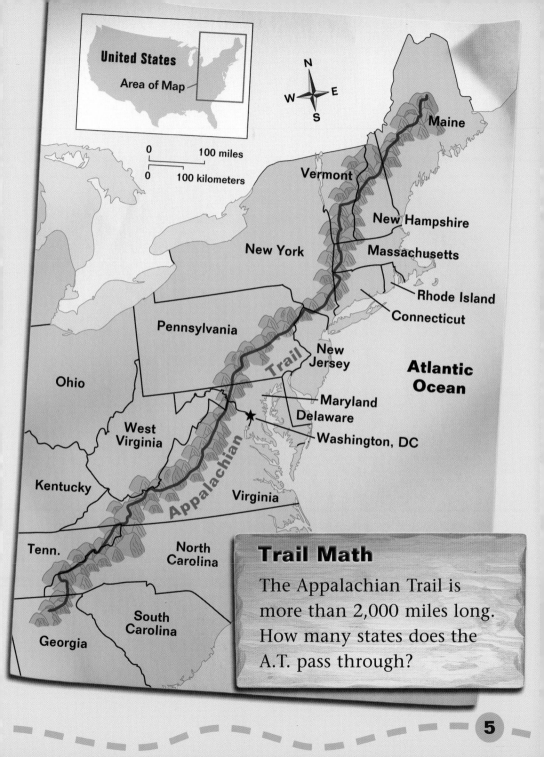

United States
Area of Map

N
W   E
S

0   100 miles
0   100 kilometers

Maine

Vermont

New Hampshire

New York

Massachusetts

Rhode Island

Connecticut

Pennsylvania

New Jersey

Atlantic Ocean

Ohio

Trail

Maryland

Delaware

West Virginia

Washington, DC

Appalachian

Kentucky

Virginia

Tenn.

North Carolina

Trail Math

The Appalachian Trail is more than 2,000 miles long. How many states does the A.T. pass through?

South Carolina

Georgia

A Dream Comes True

Benton MacKaye

The A.T. was the dream of Benton MacKaye. As a child in the early 1900s, MacKaye explored the woods of Massachusetts. He loved spending time outdoors. As an adult, he imagined a long trail through miles of wilderness. This trail would let people escape the busy world of cars and buildings. Along the trail, hikers could enter a world of forests and mountains.

People liked MacKaye's idea. In 1922, **volunteers** in New York decided to build the first section of the trail. They dug up trees, moved rocks, and built bridges. It was a lot of work. A few years later, a man named Myron Avery joined in MacKaye's dream. He and MacKaye worked with volunteers to build the rest of the trail. The A.T. was finished in 1937.

Volunteers cleared trees to build the Appalachian Trail.

Trail Math

Volunteers began building the A.T. in 1922. This trail was finished in 1937. How many years did it take to build the Appalachian Trail?

Packing for the Trip

Many people hike for just one day along the Appalachian Trail. Some people hike the whole trail. When people hike in the wilderness, they need to pack carefully. They need a lot of food and water. They need to be ready for cold or rainy weather. A.T. hikers carry their backpacks for miles and miles, so they try to make their packs light.

Here are some of the things a hiker might pack.

Tent

Sleeping bag

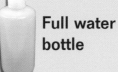
Full water bottle

Clothes

Food

Rain jacket

Stove

Things to Pack	Weight
Tent	7 pounds
Sleeping bag	4 pounds
Backpack	6 pounds
Stove	2 pounds
Clothes	3 pounds
Full water bottle	5 pounds
Food	3 pounds
Rain jacket	2 pounds

Trail Math

How much would a backpack full of these things weigh?

Backpack

The Journey Begins

Each spring more than a thousand hikers begin to walk the A.T. Most of them start at Springer Mountain in Georgia. Their hike may be difficult. It could last for more than six months! Not everyone will make it all the way to Maine. The hikers tie their boots and load their packs on their backs. Then they begin.

Hikers find their way by reading maps and following signs. They also follow **white blazes**. These white rectangles are painted on trees and rocks.

The A.T. has special signs and white blazes to help hikers follow the trail.

Trail Names

Red Owl, Pooh, Eagle, Carolina Cooker, the Singing Horseman. What are these names? When hikers meet, they give each other **trail names**, or nicknames. After a few weeks on the trail, hikers learn each other's trail names and become good friends.

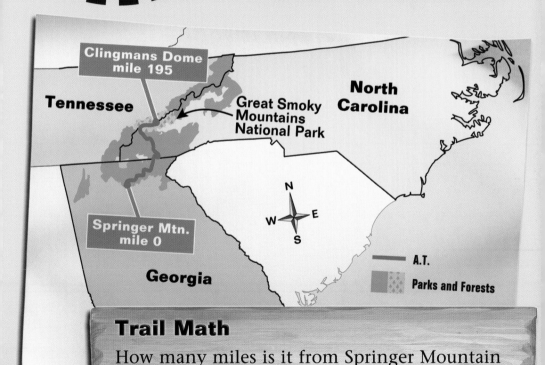

Clingmans Dome
mile 195

Tennessee

North
Carolina

Great Smoky
Mountains
National Park

N
W E
S

Springer Mtn.
mile 0

Georgia

A.T.

Parks and Forests

Trail Math

How many miles is it from Springer Mountain to Clingmans Dome?

After hiking for about one or two weeks, the A.T. hikers reach the Smoky Mountains. Here the trail is very **steep** and rocky. It is almost straight up and down in spots. Hikers walk up the steep sides of the mountains. Imagine climbing stairs for hours! By the time hikers reach the Shenandoah Mountains in Virginia, many are too excited by the beautiful views to think of their sore muscles.

Rain clouds can make these mountains look smoky.

There are **hazards**, or dangers, along the way. In the summer one hazard is the heat. Carrying a backpack a long way can be very hard when it's hot. Hikers need to drink a lot of water, or they become tired or sick. Sometimes it's hard to find water when there is not a lot of rain.

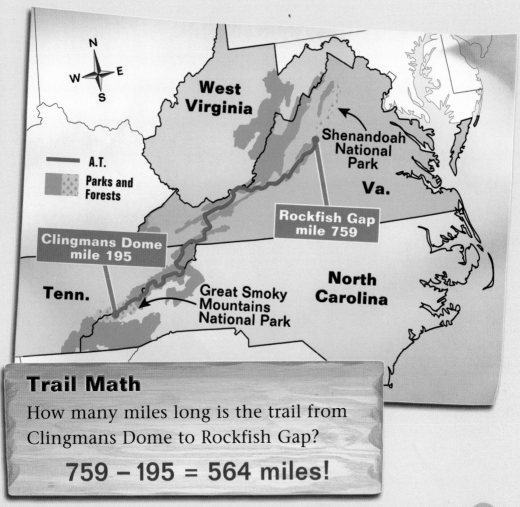

N
W E
S

West Virginia

Shenandoah National Park

Va.

A.T.

Parks and Forests

Rockfish Gap
mile 759

Clingmans Dome
mile 195

North Carolina

Tenn.

Great Smoky Mountains National Park

Trail Math

How many miles long is the trail from Clingmans Dome to Rockfish Gap?

$$759 - 195 = 564 \text{ miles!}$$

Hikers share the trail with deer, foxes, black bears, and other animals. Hikers like to see the **wildlife**, but they don't want to get too close to the animals. Bears eat the hikers' food if they can find it. Before the hikers climb into their sleeping bags for a good night's rest, they hide their food in bear boxes. The boxes are locked so that bears can't open them.

Hikers might see black bears along parts of the A.T.

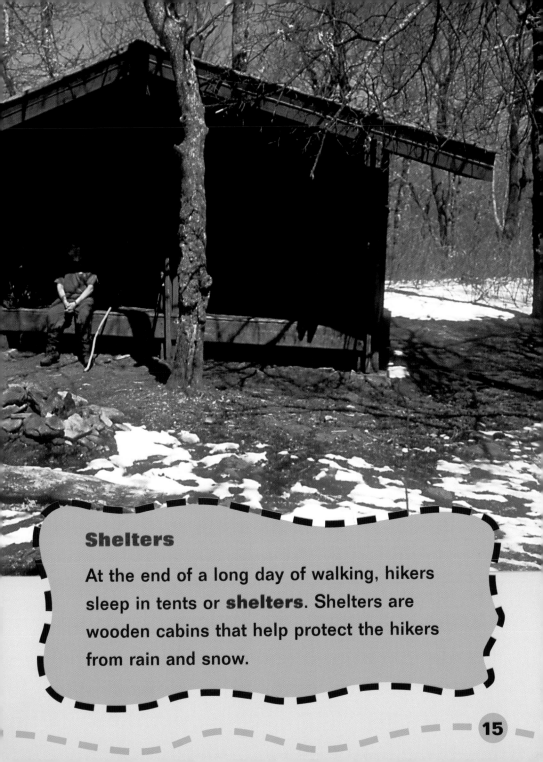

Shelters

At the end of a long day of walking, hikers sleep in tents or **shelters**. Shelters are wooden cabins that help protect the hikers from rain and snow.

Rocky Peaks

After a few months, some of the hikers reach the White Mountains. These mountains are very rocky and steep. They are the highest mountains in New Hampshire. Hikers climb to the **peaks**, or tops, of the mountains. There are beautiful views all around.

The weather can be very cool in these mountains, and clouds can make it hard to see. Sometimes it even snows in the summer. Mountain weather can change quickly. Along the trail there can be sudden thunderstorms, snowstorms, hail, or heavy rain.

Hikers walk carefully over the rocks on these mountains in New Hampshire.

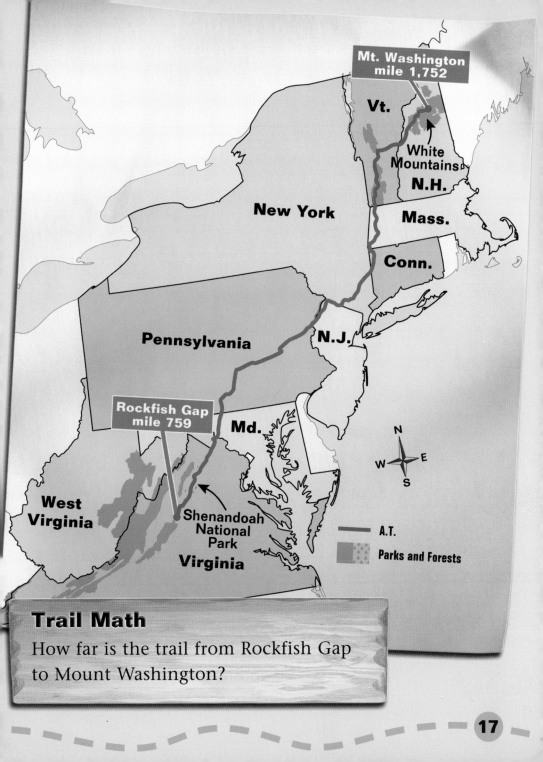

Mt. Washington
mile 1,752

Vt.

White
Mountains

N.H.

New York

Mass.

Conn.

Pennsylvania

N.J.

Rockfish Gap
mile 759

Md.

N
W — E
S

West
Virginia

Shenandoah
National
Park

——— A.T.

Parks and Forests

Virginia

Trail Math

How far is the trail from Rockfish Gap
to Mount Washington?

The tallest mountain in New Hampshire is Mount Washington. It has a weather station on top. Hikers might stop here to have a snack and learn about the White Mountains.

The world's strongest winds are recorded at this weather station on top of Mount Washington.

Trail Angels

As the hikers get tired and sore, they need friends to help them. Sometimes people who live near the trail surprise hikers with a treat. These people are called **trail angels**. They might wait by the trail with a bag of apples or an icy soda. Or they might drive hikers into town to buy more food.

Nearing the End

After months of walking trails and climbing over rocks and mountains, hikers reach Baxter State Park in Maine. This park is far from any city. The night sky is full of stars. In this wilderness, hikers often see moose and bears.

One night an A.T. hiker heard a noise coming from the woods in front of her. She shined her flashlight into the bushes, only to find a giant moose standing five feet away! It was scary, but it was one of her favorite moments on the trail.

Moose are the largest animals a hiker might see on the trail.

Baxter State Park is extra special because it is the end point of the whole trail. How does it feel to finish hiking more than 2,000 miles? Hikers feel very happy and tired at the same time! Their climb to the peak of Mount Katahdin in Baxter State Park can be difficult, but rewarding.

That's Amazing!

The oldest person to finish all 2,172 miles was 86 years old. The youngest hiker to complete the A.T. was only six years old! In 1993, Bill Erwin, who is blind, hiked the entire A.T. with his seeing-eye dog.

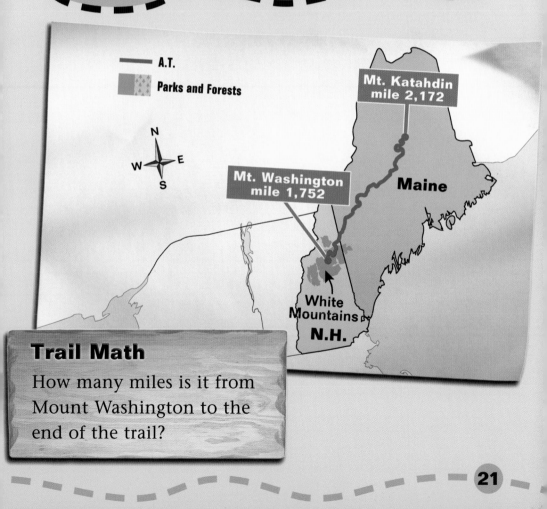

A.T.
Parks and Forests

N
W E
S

Mt. Katahdin
mile 2,172

Mt. Washington
mile 1,752

Maine

White
Mountains
N.H.

Trail Math

How many miles is it from Mount Washington to the end of the trail?

People come from all over the world to hike the Appalachian Trail. You can join in the adventure, too. Wherever the A.T. crosses a road, you can start hiking. Or you can be a volunteer who works on the trail. You can be a trail angel. People of all ages are always welcome to join in the great A.T. adventure. One day you might walk the whole trail!

People of all ages can walk the Appalachian Trail.

Glossary

footpath	a path where people can walk
hazard	something that is dangerous
hike	to take a long walk, usually through the woods
mountain range	a group of mountains
peak	the highest point of a mountain
shelter	a small cabin or other place where hikers sleep at night
steep	almost straight up and down
trail angel	a person who surprises a hiker with a treat
trail name	a nickname that hikers give one another
volunteer	someone who helps out without being paid
white blaze	a white rectangle on a tree or rock
wilderness	a natural area far from cities and towns
wildlife	animals living in their natural surroundings

Index